Love from the sky

Seamond and the Flying Santa

Written by Angeli Perrow
Illustrated by Heidi Farrow

For lighthouse children everywhere
- A.P.

For Dana, Autumn and Thea. . . and thank you to Elizabeth and Charlie
- H.F.

Book layout by Michele Bonin
www.michelebonin.com

A little red plane circled the island lighthouse. Three packages dropped from the sky. . .

one on the lawn,

one in the pond,

one on a rock. . .

and the Flying Santa waved goodbye.

Seamond remembered that moment well — the moment every lighthouse child dreamed of throughout the year. Her heart skipped with excitement. Wonderful gifts nestled in the packages— candy and pinwheels, puzzles and magazines, ribbons and bows, and always a new book by Mr. Snow, the Flying Santa himself, signed with his big, sprawling signature.

Her mother had helped her write a letter to him requesting a special gift.

It lay inside the last package, the one that hit the rock – a beautiful china doll. But it was no longer beautiful – it was broken.

Tears slid down Seamond's cheeks. "Poor Molly," she whispered.

July 1946

S	M	T	W	T	F	S
		1	2	3	4	5	6
7	8	9	10	11	12	13
14	15	16	17	18	19	20
21	22	23	24	25	26	27
28	29	30	31			

Her father made a sling for the little doll's arm and Seamond patched her head with band-aids.

Now she hugged Molly and stared at the calendar. December seemed so far away. What would Santa bring her this time? Would it land safely on the lawn? Or would it land in the pond and be sea-swamped? Or worse yet, would it hit the ground and break like Molly?

Every time she heard a plane, Seamond asked, "Is that him? Is that my Santa?"
"No, my dear," her mother would reply, "it's only July. Stay busy and the time will fly."
"Come, Molly, come Rex," Seamond said with a sigh, "we've work to do."

They collected eggs in the henhouse and pulled weeds in her little garden.

Seamond helped her father polish the brass in the lantern room. She watched him trim the wicks and fill the tank with fuel. Together they watched the sun sink into the western sea. Her father lit the lamp and the tower filled with golden light.

The sun rose on another day of adventure. Seamond rowed to the tiny island where the Monument stood in memory of an early explorer from England. "I, Bartholomew Gosnold, claim this island in the name of the Queen!" she declared.

Rex, her loyal subject, barked in agreement. He taught her how to dog paddle in the pond. He was an expert teacher.

The buzz of a small plane caught her ears.
"Is that him? Is that my Santa?"
Rex and Molly looked hopeful, too.
The plane flew on by and no packages fell from the sky.

"Stay busy and time will fly," Seamond told her buddies with a sigh. "Come, Molly, come, Rex, we've magic to make."

Seamond climbed the
s
p
i
r
a
l
s
t
a
i
r
s
of the tower to the catwalk. She
was Rapunzel letting down her
golden hair, even though her
hair was short and brown.

"Slay me a dragon, fair Prince!"
she commanded.

Rex waved his white tail and
trotted away. He returned with
a dead fish and laid it at her feet.

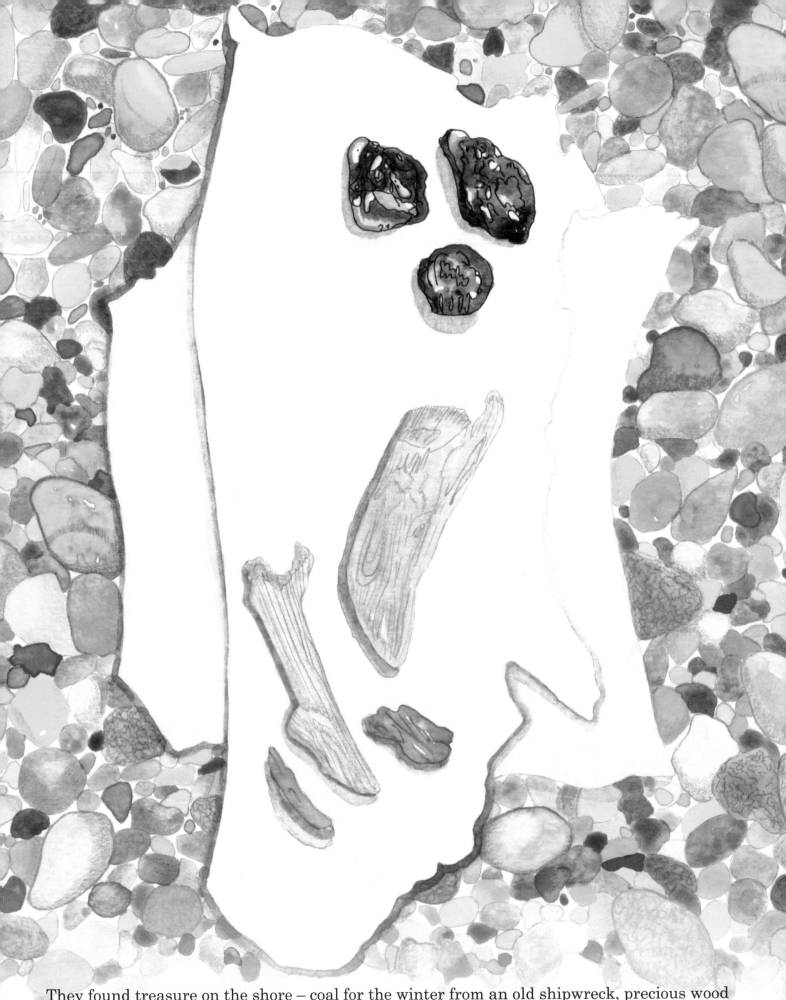

They found treasure on the shore – coal for the winter from an old shipwreck, precious wood for her father's model ships, pieces of cowhide for a weatherproof roof on the chicken coop.

She watched her father take lobsters from his underwater pen to carry to the house. Their claws clicked and clacked in the bottom of the boat.

Seamond's eyes strayed to the sky. "Where, oh where, are you, my Santa?" she said.

The sky gleamed an empty blue. "Come, Molly, come, Rex, we've exploring to do."

Seamond gathered strawberries on Morning Glory Hill and the three friends sat in a hidey hole in the tall grass, eating them until their mouths turned red.

"Rex, it's time for Molly to have a checkup."

Seamond laid the doll in the soft grass and checked her heart with her pretend stethoscope. She carefully removed the old sling and replaced it with a clean piece of white cloth. Old band-aids, soiled and rumpled, were peeled off and new ones pressed on to cover the cracks in Molly's head.

"Good as new. . . almost," Dr. Seamond announced. "Be sure to take it easy – no running, no jumping."

The thrum of a plane buzzed in the distance.

"Is that him? Is that my Santa?"

Seamond grabbed Molly and ran for the house. When she got there, the plane had flown on by and no packages had dropped from the sky.

Her parents stood in the doorway, a letter in her father's hand. Her mother's eyes were red and watery. "We have news," her father said, sadness in his voice. "We're leaving Cuttyhunk."

On a day in September, her father locked the door of the lighthouse for the first time. They had never needed a key before. The lighthouse was condemned and would be torn down.

"Poor lighthouse," Seamond said, "you've done nothing wrong. Why should you be punished?" And then another thought struck her. How would Santa find her if they moved?

At West Chop Light on Martha's Vineyard, Seamond went to school. She rode a bike with Molly in the basket and Rex loping behind. She missed the wonderful world of Cuttyhunk, but liked her new life, too. Her only worry: Would Santa find her?

A plane flew over and Seamond raced out of the house to see. But the plane flew on by and no packages dropped from the sky.

As December approached, she got up the courage to ask her father.

"No," he said, "Mr. Snow won't be flying here.'

Seamond couldn't believe her ears. The Flying Santa wasn't coming? How could that be? She was still a lighthouse girl. Her father was still a lighthouse keeper. Her heart was sad. No more wonderful packages from the sky.

"If we were still at Cuttyhunk, Santa would find us," she told Molly and Rex.

A few days before Christmas, the house filled with delicious smells of balsam fir and baking cookies. The tree stood in the parlor, decorated with old ornaments her mother had gathered over the years, little flags of different countries, tinsel and angel hair.

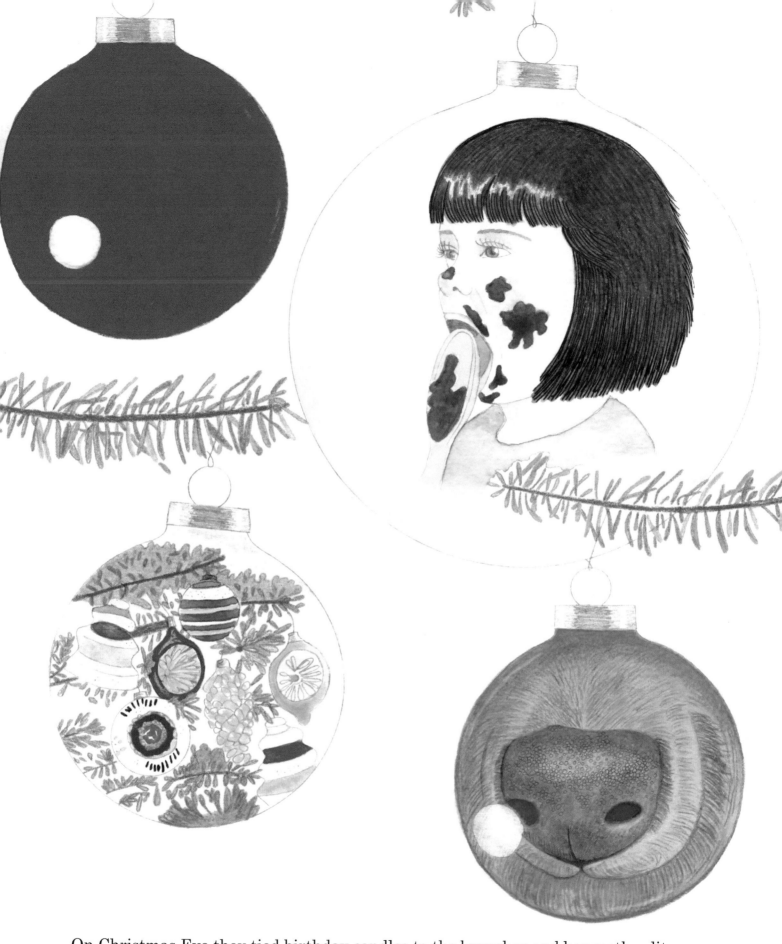

On Christmas Eve they tied birthday candles to the branches and her mother lit them. Her father stood by with the fire extinguisher. For a few moments the tree glowed with magic glory and then her father snuffed the candles out.

On Christmas Day, her mother said, "Get your coat and boots, hat and mittens. We're going to the Gay Head Lifesaving Station for a visit."

A lot of people milled around, talking and laughing. Seamond wondered why they were all outside on such a cold day. She shivered in her boots and hugged Molly close. A strange noise filled the air – thrump, thrump, thrump. A helicopter, like a giant mosquito, landed on the lawn.

Out jumped the Flying Santa with a bundle in his hands. "Special delivery for Seamond," he called. Her mother gently took Molly from her and pushed her forward. Her Santa placed a beautiful new doll in her arms. "Your mother wrote me a letter and told me what happened to your Christmas doll last year," he explained. "I wanted you to have a new one and I wanted to make sure it reached you in one piece!"

Doll and all, Seamond hugged him. Her Santa. The man who kept his promise and delivered love from the sky.

"Don't worry, Molly," she whispered. "We have Polly now but I will always love you, too."

Seamond Ponsart with her parents and "Flying Santa"
Edward Rowe Snow on December 12, 1946

Seamond's Flying Santa was Edward Rowe Snow, famous historian and author. Every year at Christmas time, Mr. Snow — with the help of his wife and daughter -- dressed in his red Santa suit and delivered care packages to lighthouse families and U.S. Coast Guard stations in New England as a way of saying "thank you" for the important job they did to keep mariners safe. The tradition was started in 1929 by Bill Wincapaw, a pilot in Maine who carried on the flights for many years with the assistance of his wife and son. The visits were a high point of the year for the lighthouse children.

Flying Santa flights are continued today by a nonprofit organization, Friends of Flying Santa, as a way of expressing appreciation to Coast Guard families who keep watch over our coastal waters. Each December, Flying Santa flies to 32 locations from Maine to New York, delivering gifts to more than 1000 children from 50 Coast Guard units. To learn more, visit www.flyingsanta.org.

Flying Santa at Chatham Light in Massachusetts
Photo by Brian Tague

Authors' Note

Seamond Ponsart, a lightkeeper's daughter, lived at Cuttyhunk Light off Cape Cod, Massachusetts, in the 1940s. The west end of the island, where her family lived, was desolate and isolated, and they felt like pioneers. When Seamond was nearly seven, she and her family moved to West Chop Light on Martha's Vineyard. It seemed like a luxury to live in a place with electricity, running water, and a real bathroom, instead of an outhouse!

Rex, the white retriever with floppy ears, was Seamond's constant companion at Cuttyhunk. He lives on in her memory as her hero dog and best buddy.

My sincere thanks go to Jeremy D'Entremont, lighthouse historian and author, for bringing Seamond's wonderful story to me after he had already done extensive interviews and research. To learn more about Seamond's remarkable life, read the book she and Jeremy have co-authored, *Everyday Heroes: The True Story of a Lighthouse Family*.

A huge thank-you also goes to Brian Tague, president of Friends of the Flying Santa, for his support in having this book published. You can find out more about the history and present-day mission of this organization by visiting www.flyingsanta.org.